God's Celestial

NETWORK

GARY C. PRICE & TANICIA PRIOLEAU

God's Celestial Network
Omega Church and Ministries Center
P.O. Box 960146
Riverdale, GA 30296
www.omegaministries.org
ISBN: 978-0-9714797-4-6
Printed in the United States of America.
Remnant Publishing House,
Atlanta, GA 30122

Contents

Acknowledgment

Understanding God's Celestial Network has been a special blessing. When we began to write this book, it allowed us to understand the greatness of our God. We are thankful to God for the ability to see the vision and produce it within the pages of this book.

We want to thank Omega Church and Ministries Center, Inc. for the faithfulness, prayer, and support you continue to provide; because of your prayers and support, we have all worked together as a great T-E-A-M, remembering that Together, Each Accomplishes More.

Thanks to everyone for your support and love. May the pages of this book be a special blessing to you.

Meet The Authors

Gary C. Price

Pastor Gary C. Price is the Senior Pastor of Omega Church and Ministries Center located in Atlanta, Georgia. He ministers to the Body of Christ under an anointing that deals specifically with the bondage of the inner man.

Pastor Price believes that the present-day church has lost the vision that Jesus Christ imparted to the Apostles before He departed to be enthroned with His Father. He also received the revelations of a prophetic voice calling the Church back to patriarchal authority and obedience to the Holy Spirit when listening to his words.

His ministry began in 1984 after God prophetically called him to remove barriers that Satan has constructed to separate God from His people. The main obstacle to be removed, he believes, is religious bondage to man-centered organizations. Therefore, he has diligently sought the Lord for guidance on how to go about initiating the end-time deliverances to set the Body of Christ free.

Tanicia Prioleau

Tanicia Prioleau enjoys writing regularly for the "Manifested Sons" blog site. She has enjoyed writing since her youth. An intercessor, wife, and mother of two children, she spends her days sharing and ministering the word of God and working in the field of Information Technology with over fourteen years of experience.

Tanicia was raised in the church and began to walk in the religious tradition of men. She always identified as a devout Christian, but she had no real commitment to the Lord Jesus Christ.

While walking in the perversion and ways of the world, she encountered an evangelist who informed her that "You must be born again." These words were new to her as she previously learned that she would always be saved once she was saved; however, this turned out to be false. After a prayer of repentance, the Lord Jesus Christ saved Tanicia and began to open the scriptures of the Bible to her.

From that time, she has learned about Jesus Christ and is transforming from religious traditions to a relationship with Jesus. Through the ministry of reconciliation, she is being led back to God the Father, understanding what it truly means to be a Child of God. She endeavors to lead others to Jesus through writing, teaching, and any tool God may use to spread His gospel of the Kingdom.

Foreword

God's Celestial Network is truly a must-read for all end-times saints looking to be both edified and equipped to engage in productive spiritual warfare. From babes in Christ to mature believers, this book serves as an invaluable tool to deepen and illuminate our understanding of God's Kingdom and Satan's plans to hinder our progress in it.

Jesus often used agricultural terminology and context to reveal the mysteries of the Gospel to followers during His time. So likewise, He has empowered Pastor Price and Sis. Tanicia, through the Holy Spirit, to unveil the mysteries of the Gospel and His Kingdom using technical terminology and context for believers of today's information age. It has been a blessing to witness how the Lord has used them to deliver this content for the body of Christ.

The revelation within these pages will undoubtedly challenge you to examine yourself and where you stand as it relates to God's Celestial Network taking steps to draw closer to Him. The Lord desires that you plug into His Kingdom like never before as we near the end of this age. This book is a vital tool to help you do just that.

—Danielle Washington

INTRODUCTION

THE REVELATION OF GOD'S CELESTIAL NETWORK TESTIMONY

It was August 2021 when God revealed His celestial network. As the world was on a lockdown due to the COVID-19 pandemic, Pastor Gary Price also fought the battle against this virus for ten days. The prayer of the saints and God's faithfulness helped Pastor Price overcome COVID. In God's word, we read that He will draw near to us if we draw near to God. We believe through the continual fervent prayers, God brought healing during those trying times.

While in the hospital, God showed Pastor Price several revelations regarding the celestial network. First, the Lord began to visit Pastor Price at night through divine revelation. While struggling to breathe on four liters of oxygen, the Lord Jesus Christ helped him breathe and overcome. After this visitation, Pastor Price was not the same. God realigned his mind with Him, his priorities were heavenly, and the old man was being put to death. He left the hospital as a vessel more fit to help others get saved and set free from the devil's bondage.

We are thankful for the Lord Jesus Christ and his miracle-working power. He is the only one that can keep and protect us as we abide under the shadow of His wings. We pray God will give you understanding through His word regarding His heavenly network and bring you back in alignment with Him.

CHAPTER 1

INTRODUCTION TO THE CELESTIAL NETWORK

> *"For as the body is one and hath many members, and all the members of that one body, being many, are one body: so also is Christ. For by one Spirit are we all baptized into one body, whether we be Jews or Gentiles, whether we be bond or free; and have been all made to drink into one Spirit.*
>
> *For the body is not one member, but many. If the foot shall say, Because I am not the hand, I am not of the body; is it therefore not of the body? And if the ear shall say, Because I am not the eye, I am not of the body; is it therefore not of the body? If the whole body were an eye, where were the hearing? If the whole were hearing, where were the smelling? But now hath God set the members every one of them in the body, as it hath pleased him."*
>
> **—1 Corinthians 12:12–18**

As stated in the scripture, we are a body made of many members. We are all created for a purpose. Man is one of God's greatest creations; we are fearfully and wonderfully made. *Psalms 139:*

Nothing God has created is without meaning; we all have a divine purpose while here on earth.

Our bodies consist of three parts: body, soul, and spirit. If we examine the human body carefully, we will notice similarities between the human body and a computer. Firstly, we must understand some of the primary components of a computer:

CPU (Central processing unit): The central processing unit is the computer's brain. Every input and operation that you do with your computer is processed. It receives instructions, processes them, and delivers an output.

Hard Drives: The hard drive is where all your pictures, videos, and document programs are stored. It permanently stores data on your computer, meaning the files stored would not disappear every time you shut down and reboot your computer. Hard drives can be internal or external.

Random Access Memory (RAM): Random Access Memory is high-speed storage where your computer and its programs can temporarily store common data that programs constantly use. Unlike the hard drives that store data permanently, RAM disposes of data stored in it when you turn off your computer. The more memory your RAM can store, the more programs you can run simultaneously. As a result, most people prefer computers with bigger RAM, as RAM size is a huge factor in computer speed.

These are a few components, amongst others. Comparing our body to these components, at a high-level view, our three-part being can be seen as Physical Body (*Hardware*), Soul (*Software*), and spirit (*the power supply*). Our body is conscious of this 3D world, our soul is self-conscious, and the spirit is God-conscious.

As we begin to understand the supernatural celestial network of God, we will notice how the members of our body are designed to work in perfect harmony. This book aims to recalibrate your mind; wherever the soul is mentioned in this writing, it includes your mind, will, and emotions. Recalibration will reset the software of your soul, giving you a renewed mind that the Spirit of God can now lead. Once this optimization takes place, you will become a manifested Son of God.

> *"For as many as are led by the Spirit of God, they are the sons of God."*
>
> **—Romans 8:14 KJV**

Recalibration is done to correct a device; this is normally done via a system reset. Optimization is the modifying of a system to make it work more efficiently. As you read, it is my prayer that the word of God will reset your mind to understand the will of God, which will cause you to become the will of God, operating efficiently to achieve maximum productivity with no wasted effort.

Understanding the Network

A network is a group or system of interconnected people or things. A network (in computer networking) is two or more connected computers that can communicate and transmit data.

When we speak of a network, it is likened to the network in your home or office. Whether you connect via a wireless (Wi-Fi) connection or an Ethernet cable, this connection allows your device to access the internet.

When God created man in His image, He directly designed us to connect to him and dwell with Him in His celestial network or kingdom. The word "Kingdom" refers to a territory or realm subject to the rule of a King. Heaven is the spiritual abode of God; it is His royal domain. God is the creator of the celestial network.

This is revealed in the story of creation outlined in the first chapter of Genesis.

"In the beginning, God created the heavens and the earth; the earth was formless and void; it was a waste and empty. Darkness was upon the face of the deep, and the _primeval_ ocean covered the unformed earth.

The Spirit of God hovered over the face of the waters, and with His creative power, God spoke, "Let there be light," and there was light. God saw that the light was good, suitable, and pleasant. So He approved it, and God distinguished the light from the darkness.

God continued making the firmament (the heavens/sky) and the dry land (earth). Earth was able to bring forth grass, herb, yielding seed, and the fruit tree yielding fruit after its kind. God saw this was good, and His word sustained it. He continued to make every living creature after its kind; it was good."

—Genesis 1

"After God created the heavens, wild animals, etc., God said, 'Let Us (Father, Son, Holy Spirit) make man in Our Image, according to Our likeness; and let them have complete authority over the entire earth (domain).'"

—Genesis 1:26

"So God created man in His Image and Likeness. He made male and female. He blessed them, granting them authority, and said, 'Be fruitful, multiply and fill the earth (realm).'"

God created man with His spiritual personality and moral likeness, allowing mankind to have His divine nature as such Adam & Eve had unbroken communion with God. Adam & Eve reflected the perfect image of God (*sinlessness*). They were both in a state of innocence with the ability to enjoy intimate fellowship and harmony with the Father as they continued to dwell in His celestial (*heavenly*) network.

Everything was made in God's perfect design. Adam communicated directly with God because he dwelled in His heavenly kingdom.

As the Creator, God's mind is comparable to a mainframe computer. A mainframe computer combines many processors and memory (RAM). The mainframe works as a central processing unit for many workstations and terminals connected to it. It can allow thousands of users to connect simultaneously. Its name "Mainframe" describes a frame for holding several processors and main memory.

Adam & Eve had access to everything in the Garden of Eden because they remained connected to the mind of God, the "Mainframe." As a result, they also had dominion in the earthly realm. His creation was operating perfectly until the serpent inserted a virus.

The Serpent Virus

> *"Now the Serpent was more subtil than any beast of the field which the LORD God had made. And he said unto the woman, Yea, hath God said, Ye shall not eat of every tree of the Garden? And the woman said unto the Serpent, We may eat of the fruit of the trees of the Garden: but of the fruit of the tree which is in the midst of the Garden, God hath said, Ye shall not eat of it, neither shall ye touch it, lest ye die. And the Serpent said unto the woman, Ye shall not surely die: for God doth know that in the day ye eat thereof, then your eyes shall be opened, and ye shall be as gods, knowing good and evil."*
>
> **—Genesis 3:1–5**

Eve encountered a whispering serpent while in the Garden. This Serpent was more crafty, subtle, and skilled in deceit than any living creature of the field which the Lord had made. The Serpent spoke to the woman about the validity of God's word (command).

18

God gave a command to Adam to eat fruit freely from every tree of the Garden except the tree of the knowledge (recognition) of good and evil; otherwise, on the day he eats from it, he will most certainly die. *Gen 2* (emphasis added)

Through his devious and cunning words, the Serpent (Satan) began to sow seeds of doubt into the mind of Eve. These words introduced a virus into God's creation.

A virus is a malicious code or program written to alter how a computer operates. In this case, the Serpent introduced words (a virus) to alter Eve's operation, and most importantly, what she thought about God. A virus is also designed to spread from one computer to another; hence, Eve, after she gave heed to the Serpent's words, influenced Adam to receive the serpent's virus.

A virus operates by inserting or attaching itself into a rightful program or document supporting macros to execute its code. The serpent's virus inserted and attached itself to the rightful rulers of the earthly domain. This eventually led to the fall of man.

The Fall of Man (*A hacked mind*)

"*And when the woman saw that the tree was good for food and that it was pleasant to the eyes, and a tree to be desired to make one wise, she took of the fruit thereof, and did eat, and gave also unto her husband with her; and he did eat.*

And the eyes of them both were opened, and they knew that they were naked, and they sewed fig leaves together, and made themselves aprons."

And they heard the voice of the LORD God walking in the Garden in the cool of the day: and Adam and his wife hid themselves from the presence of the LORD God amongst the trees of the Garden. And the LORD God called unto Adam, and said unto him, Where art thou?"

—Genesis 3:6–9

After receiving the words of the whispering Serpent, Eve began to believe the lie of Satan. She initially received the download of the devil's words. However, the serpent's virus introduced several contagions into her system. These contagions operate like biological viruses, which can transfer from host to host; contagion is a disease or contamination spread by close contact.

Satan sowed seeds of discontentment and covetousness into her heart. As a result, Eve began to long for what was forbidden.

Discontentment opened the door to covetousness, which caused Eve to lust. She became overtaken by the lust of the flesh, eyes, and pride of life. One virus introduced via words produced several contagions in the body of Eve.

- She saw the tree was good for food- *Lust of the Flesh*
- The tree was pleasant to the eyes – *Lust of the Eyes*
- She noticed the tree was desirable to make her wise and insightful – *Pride of Life*

> *"For all that is in the world, the lust of the flesh, and the lust of the eyes, and the pride of life, is not of the Father but is of the world."*

1 John 2:16 KJV

Eve succumbed to the temptation of the Serpent, which caused her to take the fruit and eat it. Her husband ate some as well. The Serpent tempted Eve, and in return, she tempted Adam to eat from the tree. This virus attacked the mind by distorting (perverting) God's word and causing Eve to question it. This serpent's virus probed and spread using questions that Satan introduced into Eve's mind.

Adam & Eve were both infected with the virus and its contagions. The Serpent hacked God's perfect creation. He gained illegal access to God's devices (Adam & Eve) while connected to God's celestial network by using lies spread by words.

In computer networking, when a device is infected, it must be removed from the network. Any infected device can infect other devices. Eve was infected, and she led Adam to become infected as well.

"After the fall, Adam & Eve had the nature of the Serpent. Satan had become their Father, their understanding of God was darkened, and they became alienated from the life of God through ignorance." (*Eph 4:18*). The Serpent designed this hack to defile God's created order.

Hacking attempts to exploit a computer system or a private network. When a system is exploited, the hacker has unauthorized access to or control over the system for unlawful purposes.

When a device is hacked, the data can become corrupt and manipulated. The same concept applies spiritually to God's creation. For example, when Adam & Eve were hacked, their minds became exploited and corrupted while plugged into God's celestial network due to the unauthorized access of the Serpent.

The Serpent Nature (elimination from the celestial network)

"Ye are of your Father the devil, and the lusts of your Father ye will do. He was a murderer from the beginning, and abode not in the truth, because there is no truth in him. When he speaketh a lie, he speaketh of his own: for he is a liar, and the Father of it."

—John 8:44;

After receiving the serpent's virus & nature, Adam & Eve began to act contrary to their created design. Their eyes were opened, their awareness was increased, and they knew they were naked, causing them to become self-conscious and self-aware. Self is the manifestation of a contagion introduced into our system. Instead of communing with God, the man and his wife hid and kept themselves hidden from the presence of God. Sin causes us to hide from God because sin separates us from God.

"Behold, the Lord's hand is not so short That it cannot save, Nor His ear so impaired That it cannot hear. But your wickedness has separated you from your God, And your sins have hidden His face from you so that He does not hear."

—Isaiah 59:1–2

God was walking in the Garden looking for Adam & Eve while they hid among the trees of the Garden. The Lord God called to Adam and said, "Where are you?" Their sin of disobedience caused them to disconnect from God's celestial network. As a result, God began to ask where Adam was. He was no longer freely communing with God, but he had become estranged from his creator. Sin caused Adam & Eve to hide in darkness. When God confronted Adam about hiding from his presence, Adam did not take responsibility for his sin. He began to blame GOD and the woman. In return, the woman blamed the Serpent. Neither the man nor the woman took accountability for their sin; they shifted their sin to someone else.

Blame shifting was a part of the virus, and self-preservation was the contagion. The Serpent's nature always manifests via selfishness.

- Self-awareness
- Self-consciousness
- Self-preservation
- Self-centeredness

Selfishness is a self-centered concern for oneself without due regard to the needs of others. Their eyes were open as the Serpent promised, but they were aware of themselves; they weren't God-conscious; instead, their minds became darkened. Adam & Eve were no longer illuminated in the light of God. His Glory (Holy Presence) was foreign to them, which caused self-consciousness; they were exposed to darkness.

Adam and Eve's lack of accountability nor acknowledgment of their sin led to pride. Pride and self-awareness are the nature of the Serpent; where there is pride, there is always rebellion. As Satan became their father, his rebellious nature transferred to them.

Their father, the Devil

"Where wast thou when I laid the foundations of the earth? Declare, if thou hast understanding. Who hath laid the measures thereof, if thou knowest? Or who hath stretched the line upon it? Whereupon are the foundations thereof fastened? Or who laid the cornerstone thereof; When the morning stars sang together, And all the sons of God shouted for joy?"

—Job 38:4–7

God is a Progenitor; a **Progenitor** is the founder of a family, line of descent, clan or tribe, noble house, or ethnic group. God is the creator of all things, including Angelic beings. When God created the physical universe, the sons of God shouted for joy.

Angels are celestial beings; God's Heavenly Host can be dispatched to deliver a message, bring protection, encourage, give guidance, bring punishment, patrol the earth, and fight against evil forces.

Lucifer was a higher-ranking angel, a Cherubim whose purpose was to magnify the righteousness and sovereignty of God. Their other responsibility, according to scripture, is to glorify God; they show the power and glory of God and His lasting presence.

In the book of Ezekiel and Isaiah, we begin to understand Lucifer's fall from God's heavenly kingdom.

> *"Son of man, take up a lamentation upon the king of Tyrus, and say unto him, Thus saith the Lord GOD; Thou sealest up the sum, full of wisdom, and perfect in beauty. Thou hast been in Eden the Garden of God; every precious stone was thy covering, the sardius, topaz, and the diamond, the beryl, the onyx, and the jasper, the sapphire, the emerald, and the carbuncle, and gold: the workmanship of thy tabrets and of thy pipes was prepared in thee in the day that thou wast created. Thou art the anointed Cherub that covereth; and I have set thee so: thou wast upon the holy mountain of God; thou hast walked up and down in the midst of the stones of fire. Thou wast perfect in thy ways from the day that thou wast created, till iniquity was found in thee."*
>
> **—Ezekiel 28:12–15**

After reading these verses, it is clear that Ezekiel is describing the king of Tyre in terms that could not apply to a man. According to the scripture above, this king had the following attributes:

- He was in the Garden of Eden (*28:13*)
- Cherubim angel (The anointed Cherub) (*28:14*)
- Had access to the Holy Mountain of God (*28:14*)
- He was full of wisdom and perfect in beauty.
- He is a created being.
- **Until** *iniquity* was in him, he was cast down from heaven. (28:16,17)

A few more things we can gather from the scripture above are

- He was full of wisdom, but now he has **corrupted wisdom** (*James 3:15*)
- He was created to give GOD praise and glory, but he began to **glorify himself.**
- He became **self-exalted** (narcissistic)
- Prideful and **self-deluded.** (*James 1:22*)

When he fell, he became the opposite of what God had intended him to be and became a perversion.

Perversion: The alteration of something from its original course, meaning, or state to a distortion or corruption of what was first intended.

> *"How art thou fallen from heaven, O Lucifer, son of the morning! how art thou cut down to the ground, which didst weaken the nations! For thou hast said in thine*

> *heart,* ***I will ascend into heaven, I will exalt my throne above the stars of God:*** *I* ***will sit also upon the mount of the congregation,*** *in the sides of the north:* ***I will ascend above the heights of the clouds; I will be like the most High.***"

> **Isaiah 14:12–14;**

Like Eve, Lucifer was discontent with who God created him to be; he began to covet God's authority; his lust for praise and his desire to exalt himself above God caused him to enter into pride, which was his downfall.

We can see this same nature was in Eve after she believed the lie of the Serpent. When Lucifer fell, he became Satan, an adversary, accuser, and slanderer. Instead of glorifying God, he now deceives and seduces the entire world. Satan used this same deception and seduction to lead Adam & Eve into rebellion. As a result, they were disjointed from God's Celestial Kingdom.

When a device is disjointed, its primary naming service does not match the original domain's name with which the computers are members. For example, God created Adam and Eve with his genetic coding; their coding became corrupt after their fall. As a result, Adam and Eve were driven out of the Garden because they became the opposite of God's creation.

> "*And the LORD God said, Behold, the man is become as one of us, to know good and evil: and now, lest he put forth his hand, and take also of the tree of life, and eat,*

and live forever: therefore the LORD God sent him forth from the Garden of Eden, to till the ground from whence he was taken. So he drove out the man, and he placed at the east of the Garden of Eden Cherubims, and a flaming sword which turned every way, to keep the way of the tree of life."

Genesis 3:22–24;

The fall of man brought spiritual and physical death; this spiritual death broke the fellowship and communion mankind had previously experienced with God. As a result, Adam and Eve's authority over the earthly domain was betrayed into the hands of Satan.

CHAPTER 2

THE TERRESTRIAL NETWORK

> *"But even if our gospel is [in some sense] hidden [behind a veil], it is hidden [only] to those who are perishing; among them, the god of this world [Satan] has blinded the minds of the unbelieving to prevent them from seeing the illuminating light of the gospel of the glory of Christ, who is the image of God."*
>
> **—2 Corinthians 4:3–4 AMP**

Satan, the god of this world

The Bible mentions Satan as *"the god of this world."* After the fall, when Adam & Eve betrayed the world to him, he took dominion over the world. This means Satan is the god of this particular age on earth. For a short time, he has authority in the worldly realm. He currently rules the thoughts and deeds of the people of this age. His corrupted wisdom rules in the hearts of the unsaved. His wisdom is full of error, arrogance, and hostility to the gospel of Jesus. As a result, the gospel is hidden from many people, especially the spiritually blind, unbelieving, and perishing.

Satan's network (kingdom) is terrestrial (worldly) but spiritual. On the other hand, God's network is celestial (*heavenly*) and spiritual. With this in mind, we understand we have two opposing kingdoms, "Terrestrial vs. Celestial."

When we speak of "Terrestrial," it means existing upon the earth and being worldly, whether physically or morally. The bodies we are clothed in while in this world are considered terrestrial according to *1st Corinthians 15:40.* Therefore, every inhabitant of the earth, including men, animals, plants, and the like are in terrestrial bodies.

This terrestrial network keeps our minds earthly and meditating on worldly affairs. It also keeps us blinded and distracted by what we see. Our five senses generate it: what we see, touch, taste, smell, and hear becomes our reality. God created our bodies with these five senses to operate in this age/world. However, He firstly designed us to commune and worship with Him in the Spirit as He (God) is a Spirit.

> *"God is a Spirit: and they that worship him must worship him in spirit and in truth."*
>
> **—John 4:24 KJV**

The Hierarchy of the terrestrial network

> *"For we wrestle not against flesh and blood, but against principalities, against powers, against the rulers of the darkness of this world, against spiritual wickedness in high places."*
>
> **—Ephesians 6:12**

Satan's kingdom (network) has principalities, powers, rulers of the darkness of this world, and spiritual wickedness in high places. He has a highly organized kingdom that isn't seen in the physical. His hierarchy, according to Ephesians 6 is:

Principalities: Magistrates who hold dominions entrusted to them by Satan. They are spiritual beings in the devil's network.

Powers: Demonic spiritual beings who exert their authority or right delegated. They are high-ranking evil supernatural powers.

Rulers of the darkness: *Kosmokrator,* a world ruler, lord of the world, and the prince of this age. These are angelic or demonic powers controlling the terrestrial network. *Kósmos,* "world" and *kratéō,* "to rule," refers to Satan, demons, or fallen angels that influence the lives of worldly people. These rulers do not simply seek to lead the physical world but rather the people who inhabit the physical world. The phrase "this present darkness" means the current realm of evil or the abode of evil spirits.

Spiritual wickedness in high places: They are supernatural spirits of wickedness & iniquity. The Greek word for wickedness is *"poneria"* which means depravity, mischief, and pain-ridden evil causing harm and toil. Satan is depicted as the prince of the power of the air; therefore, these evil spirits operate in our atmosphere, causing evil and inflicting harm and sickness in people's lives.

Prince of the power of the air (Satan)

> *"And you [He made alive when you] were [spiritually] dead and separated from Him because of your transgressions and sins, in which you once walked. You were following the ways of this world [influenced by this present age], in accordance with the prince of the power of the air (Satan), the spirit who is now at work in the disobedient [the unbelieving, who fight against the purposes of God]."*
>
> **—Ephesians 2:1–2 AMP**

After the fall, our spirit is dead to the life of God. As a result, we are easily led astray by our carnal senses. Our minds become estranged from the life of God. This means spiritually; our minds have become non-participatory. A non-participatory mind is shut out from intimacy and fellowship with God. In technical terms, your cellphone, laptop, or any electronic device is useless if you cannot use the features it was originally designed to provide. Any device that operates opposite of its original intent is considered "non-participatory" as it cannot produce the desired results.

Satan is the Prince of the power of the air, and he temporarily has authority on earth to command demons and influence people's minds. The unconverted mind/soul is influenced by the ways of the world and all of its adornments. Flashy lights, worldly affairs, and the desire to become someone famous in this world are alluring to many people.

The spirit of this world is an influencing spirit. Anything that is influencing can cause those who are self-conscious to become easily controlled, manipulated, and influenced by evil. These influencing spirits are causing individuals to be transformed into the image and nature of the Serpent. The more people are transformed into the Serpent's image, the darker their minds become, and their hearts are hardened against their creator, GOD. These are the unbelievers who intentionally fight against the purposes and plans of God. Being influenced by the prince of the power of the air (Satan), the person whose mind remains unaligned with God will be led down the crooked path of witchcraft.

Witchcraft: The influencing power of the terrestrial network

"But there was a certain man, called Simon, which beforetime in the same city used sorcery, and bewitched the people of Samaria, giving out that himself was some great one: To whom they all gave heed, from the least to the greatest, saying, This man is the great power of God. And to him they had regard, because that of long time he had bewitched them with sorceries.
But when they believed Philip preaching the things concerning the kingdom of God, and the name of Jesus Christ, they were baptized, both men and women."

—Acts 8:9–12 KJV

Witchcraft is a work of the flesh; it works with the spirit of this world. One of the goals is to cause people to turn away from the pathway of righteousness. In the story with Simon the sorcerer, Simon used magic arts and spells to influence and captivate the hearts of the people of Samaria. He presented himself as a great one, which caused the people to heed him. Scripture informs us that Simon bewitched the people of Samaria with sorcery for a long time.

Witchcraft is the exercise or invocation of alleged supernatural powers to control people or events; this typically involves sorcery or magic. It is an irresistible influence or fascination with something. Witchcraft helps the spirit of this world influence, captivate, and allure people's hearts. The design of witchcraft is to keep hearts captivated and minds blinded from Jesus Christ, who is the glorious light of the gospel.

Examining the scripture in Acts chapter 8 further, we can understand how the terrestrial network blinds the minds. Magic is defined as the power to "influence" a course of events using supernatural forces. Magic causes bewitchment, amazement, mystification, and dazzlement.

"Mystify" means to cause perplex, puzzle, confuse, confound, and to make obscure or mysterious.

"Dazzled" means to blind a person, deprive of sight, amaze or overwhelm someone with impressive quality, and overpower or dim the vision by light.

Simon the magician, was an agent of Satan. He used his witchcraft to blind the people. Unfortunately, they were so impressed with his magical qualities that they lost the ability to see the error of his ways. The bewitching powers broke when they heard the truth about the kingdom of God and the authority of Jesus Christ.

When we are led by the spirit of this world and influenced by the devil's kingdom, our minds are bewitched, Jesus came to set us free from the bewitching power of witchcraft. He is a Heavenly light that is glorious and majestic, He desires that we have the veil removed from our mind to regain our spiritual vision and be filled with His Holy Spirit.

The fleshly nature

> *"Now the works of the flesh are manifest, which are these; Adultery, fornication, uncleanness, lasciviousness, Idolatry, witchcraft, hatred, variance, emulations, wrath, strife, seditions, heresies, Envyings, murders, drunkenness, revellings, and such like: of the which I tell you before, as I have also told you in time past, that they which do such things shall not inherit the kingdom of God."*
>
> **—Galatians 5:19–21 KJV**

In Satan's Terrestrial kingdom, the fleshly (carnal) nature is the driving force. The flesh is the earthly nature of man that is apart from divine (Godly) influence, and this nature is prone to sin and opposed to God. As previously mentioned, this kingdom is generated by our five carnal senses; which are all part of the flesh.

Flesh (*sarx*) is the physical body as opposed to the soul and spirit. It is what's seen externally, in computing terms, it would be considered the hardware. Our fleshly nature includes human frailties rather physically or morally with all of its passions and desires.

Our fleshly nature identifies with sensuality, which means we are inclined to fulfill pleasurable desires. This gratifies the carnal appetites. Scripture warns us that man without God is a beast (*Ecclesiastes 3:18), and* this animalistic nature is the same nature that was transferred to Adam & Eve in the garden after they received the serpent's virus.

As a result, everyone born into this world is born with a sinful nature, and when we give in to the gratifying desires of the flesh, we are made more into the image of the beast. Our animal nature is incited to sin, leading to the manifestations of the flesh listed above. Our minds can become reprobate when we continue down this road of depravity.

Corrupted files

To understand reprobation in technical terms, let's define what happens when a device experiences data corruption. First, remember, a mind that remains separated from God and His heavenly network is open to receiving corrupted data from Satan's kingdom.

Data corruption occurs when an electronic device becomes corrupted, usually caused by a corrupt/contaminated file that causes errors in the device's data during any process.

When data corruption is introduced into a device, it causes unintended changes to the original data. Some possible causes of data corruption are malware/virus infections, sudden loss of power/shut down during an operation, physical hardware issues, or any interruption in normal computer processes. Think about a time when you experienced a sudden shutdown, problems in your body, or any interruption to your normal functionality; it works the same.

In most cases, when data is corrupt, whether, on your computer, cellphone, or gaming device, there is no guarantee you will recover your files. Likewise, our minds estranged (separated) from God's will begin to degenerate; a reprobate mind doesn't desire to retain God in its knowledge. As a result, our data which is our thoughts become more corrupt, causing our files (mind) to become irretrievable.

The road to a corrupt mind

> *"Because that, when they knew God, they glorified him not as God, neither were thankful; but became vain in their imaginations, and their foolish heart was darkened.*
>
> **—Romans 1:21–32 KJV**

Professing themselves to be wise, they became fools, And changed the glory of the incorruptible God into an image made like to corruptible man, and to birds, and four footed beasts, and creeping things. Wherefore God also gave them up to **uncleanness** through the lusts of their own hearts, to dishonor their own bodies between themselves: Who changed the truth of God into a lie, and worshipped and served the creature more than the Creator, who is blessed forever. Amen.

For this cause God gave them up unto **vile affections**: for even their women did change the natural use into that which is against nature: And likewise also the men, leaving the natural use of the woman, burned in their lust one toward another; men with men working that which is unseemly, and receiving in themselves that recompense of their error which was meet. And even as they did not like to retain God in their knowledge, God gave them over to a **reprobate mind**, to do those things which are not convenient; Being filled with all unrighteousness, fornication, wickedness, covetousness, maliciousness; full of envy, murder, debate, deceit, malignity; backbiters, haters of God, despiteful, proud, boasters, inventors of evil things, disobedient to parents, without understanding, covenant-breakers, without natural affection, implacable, unmerciful: who knowing the judgment of God, that they which commit such things are worthy of death, not only do the same, but have pleasure in them that do them."

A reprobate mind is a corrupt mind. This mind has received several corrupt files into their system, which causes the person to become corrupt. These files come in via sin. As we examine Romans chapter 1, we can see how the Terrestrial network operates. The influencing spirits cause unbelief in the hearts of mankind, and while disconnected from God, the spirit of this world leads them. Many of us can identify with being led by the seducing spirit of this world; when we thought we were doing our own will, we were being led astray by Satan and his demonic hierarchy. God does not overlook sin, and His wrath is revealed against all ungodliness and unrighteousness. Walking according to the world causes the mind to suppress and stifle the truth of God. However, God designed every human with inner consciousness. Therefore, those who fail to believe and trust in God are without excuse and defense. If we fail to believe, we can become worthless, unfit, castaway, and rejected from God's celestial network eternally.

When the disobedient don't honor God or give thanks to him for his wondrous creation, they will instead become godless in their thinking, with vain imaginations and reasonings. Their minds become darkened, and when presented with the truth, their reasonings (strongholds) will defend any lie they've believed about God.

A stronghold in our mind is a spiritual fortress made up of wrong thoughts. Once a lie inserts into the mind, the devil reinforces his lies to strengthen it; this makes it a mental mindset/ stronghold designed to distort our perception of what is right and true. In (2nd Corinthians), Apostle Paul reminds us that the weapons of our warfare are not carnal but spiritual to destroy fortresses/strongholds and cast down imaginations. We cannot allow a lie or wrong thought to remain in our minds. We must learn to cast them down. Our enemy Satan has lied to us, giving us a false perception of ourselves and others around us, thoughts of inadequacy, and insufficiency, and all lies are designed to stop us from progressing in life. Like Eve believed the lie of the serpent, the veiled mind believes the lie of the influencing spirit of this world.

> *"But even if our Gospel is **veiled**, it is **veiled** to those who are perishing, whose minds the God of this age (Satan) has blinded, who do not believe, lest the light of the Gospel of the glory of Christ, who is the image of God, should shine on them."*
>
> **—2 Corinthians 4:3–4**

Continuing down this road will cause the minds to continue alienate from God. The software (minds) aren't receiving regular updates from God and will organically conform to the serpent's nature; this happens by default.

In the terrestrial network, this always leads to physical & moral defilement; where God gives this person up to uncleanness through the lust of their heart (mind). In a moral sense, uncleanness is the impurity of lustful, luxurious, and profligate living. The parable of the prodigal son is a good example of this. He desired to leave his father's house to live a wasteful and immoral lifestyle, but thanks to God, before his mind reached complete corruption, he was able to "come to himself," reasoning within his mind that he must return to his Father's house. Although the son had become prodigal (wasteful and extravagant with riotous living), he remembered His Father when he became destitute and knew he needed to return home. (*Luke 15:11-32*)

When we continue past the realm of uncleanness, it always leads to sexual immorality. We begin to dishonor our bodies. Dishonoring the body can manifest in several ways. Fornication, masturbation, pornography, adultery, marking the body (tattoos), strange piercings, etc., are all used to dishonor our bodies. In the terrestrial network, this is highly encouraged by the rulers of darkness. These influencing spirits use several media to promote sexual perversion: music, movies, social media, etc., are some of the platforms where the prince of the spirit of the air sends his influences. It is the serpent's nature to cause us to become contrary to who God created us to be; we begin to show the contrariness in our very being. Our hardware (flesh) displays our outward state of rebellion because we are plugged into a rebellious kingdom.

Due to the sexual perversion promoted in Satan's kingdom, we currently have a generation headed toward corruption. As the Apostle Paul stated, "Even the women left their natural use to lust for one another" (*Romans 1*). This is an unnatural desire; homosexuality, lesbianism, and all forms of perversion lead to a reprobate mind. The end goal of Satan's terrestrial network is to keep our minds blinded in a state of unbelief, not receiving the light of the gospel of Jesus Christ. If we continue blinded, we will have a mind completely devoid of truth, following in the ways of this present evil world and walking in darkness.

CHAPTER 3

THE HACKER

> *"And the great dragon was thrown down, the age-old serpent who is called the devil and Satan, he who continually deceives and seduces the entire inhabited world; he was thrown down to the earth, and his angels were thrown down with him."*
>
> **—Revelation 12:9 AMP**

A hacker uses a computer system to gain unauthorized access to another system for data or to make the system unavailable. These hackers will use their skills for a specific goal, such as stealing money, gaining fame by bringing down a computer system, making a network unavailable, or even sometimes, destroying them.

There are different types of hackers. We will define one description of a hacker that aligns with the deceptive nature of Satan.

Black Hat Hacker -The Evil Doer

The black hat hacker is the one who hacks with malicious intent. This type of hacker uses their skills to steal money or data, knock a computer system offline, or even destroy them. Some of these hackers love to see their work and name in the news, targeting big-name organizations and companies. For instance, they might change the front page of a company website.

Black hats also try to break into computer systems to steal credit card information and possibly steal valuable information to sell on the black market. They may even lock out the computer and network system from the owners and then hold them for ransom.

The black hat that works outside the law is the hacker we most know. Some black hats have cost companies hundreds of millions of dollars in credit cards, social security information, and theft damages. They can work as a lone wolf or with a team. They work slowly and methodically since the black hat knows it takes patience to compromise a computer or a network system to hit a big payoff and not get caught.

As we talk about hacking in spiritual terms, Satan is the master hacker. He hacked the mind of Adam & Eve using deception, and he is continually deceiving and hacking our minds daily by seducing the entire world. Everything he does is with malicious intent. Jesus warned that the thief comes to steal, kill and destroy; this is what the thief Satan does in our lives. Like the black hat hacker, he works slowly and methodically in our lives, causing trauma, rejection, and several issues to compromise our spiritual system.

> *"The thief cometh not, but for to steal, and to kill, and to destroy: I am come that they might have life and that they might have it more abundantly."*
>
> **—John 10:10 KJV**

Satan the hacker misleads people with a false appearance and lies. He leads the world into a delusion believing in his fantasies and unreality. He is a beguiler and a trickster. Our minds can be fragile; if we aren't guarding our hearts, we will be open and vulnerable for the hacker to hijack our minds. When Satan has gained illegal entry into our minds, he can implant contaminations, contagions, and defilements.

- *Contamination*: The action or state of making or being made impure by polluting or poisoning.
- *Contagion*: Rapid communication of an influence (such as a doctrine or emotional state) corrupting influence or contact.
- *Defilement*: to make physically unclean, especially with something unpleasant or contaminating.

> *"To the pure, all things are pure; but to the corrupt and unbelieving, nothing is pure; both their mind and their conscience are corrupted."*
>
> **—Titus 1:15**

Satan pollutes our minds by giving us immoral thoughts to defile our character. He causes wounds and trauma to implant his contaminations. His goal is to cause the impure pollution in our minds to remain in us and grow with us. If it is unaddressed, this pollution continues to grow, eventually becoming mental strongholds. Furthermore, his contaminations are like system viruses that can cause our minds to go offline from God. As a result, we no longer have a connection to the mind of God; this makes us open and vulnerable to Satan's contagions.

The Contagion of Sin

> *"If a man carries meat that is holy [because it has been offered in sacrifice to God] in the fold of his garment, and he touches bread, or cooked food, or wine, or oil, or any [kind of] food with this fold, does what he touches become holy [dedicated exclusively to God's service]? And the priests answered, "No!" [**Holiness is not transferrable**.] Then Haggai said, "If one who is [ceremonially] unclean because of [contact with] a corpse touches any of these [articles of food], will it be unclean?" And the priests answered, "It will be unclean." [**Ceremonial uncleanness, like sin, is infectious.**]"*
>
> **—Haggai 2:12–13 AMP**

God made it clear in Haggai chapter 2 that sin is infectious. Something infectious can transmit through people, organisms, or the environment. So the saying "one bad apple can spoil the whole bunch" is correct.

Sin spreads rapidly through communication or influence; we read in 1st Corinthians 15:33; "Be not deceived: evil communications corrupt good manners." Deception can bring corrupting influences by several means, one of which is evil communication. When we walk in deceit, we begin to roam from the path of safety, truth, or virtue. Wandering down the wrong path, we start to be out of the way of Jesus Christ. Most importantly, deception can cause us to be led away into the error of sin.

Evil (corrupt) communication with unholy companions and associations will corrupt our godly character. Corrupt communication is anything that spoils our character, ruins our morality, and defiles our being. Some examples of corrupt communications include gossip, slander, and evil speaking. The quickest way to transfer a corrupting influence is via words through direct communication, music, social mediums, etc. Most of our corrupting influences came via words. We may have experienced peer pressure as a child, listened to ungodly entertainment, the enticing words of the opposite sex, or the words designed to tear down our confidence. Either way, this exchange/communication is done via the words we speak or hear.

Words can either build up or tear down. So Jesus Christ warned in Matthew.

> *"But I say unto you, That every idle word that men shall speak, they shall give account thereof in the day of judgment. For by thy words thou shalt be justified, and by thy words thou shalt be condemned"*
>
> **—Matthew 12:36–37 KJV**

The Source Code

What Does Source Code Mean?

Source code is the set of instructions and statements written by a programmer using a computer programming language. This code is later translated into machine language by a compiler. The translated code is referred to as object code. God's word is always falling, either written literally through the Bible or spoken as the living word through His chosen vessels. God's word falls on the righteous or the unrighteous. Words create our environment. When God created the heavens and the earth, He spoke creation into existence. The universe/ages were framed and created in proper order for their intended purpose by the word of God. What we see physically is not made out of visible things (*Heb 11:3*). God commanded (willed) the world into existence. When God speaks anything into existence, He affirms and sustains it. In the book of Hebrews, chapter 1, we learn that the entire physical and spiritual universe is held together by the powerful word of God. Speaking of His Son, Jesus God says:

> *"...who, being the brightness of His glory and the express image of His person, and* **upholding all things by the word of His power,** *when He had by Himself purged our sins, sat down at the right hand of the Majesty on high..."*
>
> **—Hebrews 1:3 NKJV**

In computer programming, developers use source code to program a device. The source code instructs devices on which task to perform. For example, logging off and on or restarting a device is programmable by code.

Whether Mac, PC, smartphones, or tablets, all devices use a binary system. These instructions are programming code that instructs the machine on what to do in certain scenarios. These are commands human programmers can create using a computer programming language. As such, we are God's creation. God is likened to a computer programmer, and as His creation, we are expected to function the way God created us. Since we are born into sin and shaped (*molded*) into iniquity when we are disconnected from the mind of God, our programming is rewritten to accommodate the terrestrial kingdom. When this happens, we begin to identify with the hacker's code (words).

Contaminated Source Code

In software development, poorly written code is common. Poor written source code brings annoyance and can cause loss of customers. More dangerously, it can cause a security breach to the company. Some common causes of bad source code are coding typos, indenture failure, hard-coding passwords, etc. Some problems from bad code have a delay before the issue appears. It can contain errors and bugs only found during debugging when developing the software.

Believing the lies of the hacker Satan caused us to receive poorly written code over our lives hearing words like you're a whore, you're not good, you'll never amount to anything, etc., are poorly written code, this is why we have experienced frustration or annoyance with a loss of identity in our lives. Listening to the lies of the devil has caused many of us to walk and operate opposite of our intended purpose in life. As we continue down this path, we become open to hurt, and this is where a security breach happens within our souls.

An example of a breach is a gap in a wall, barrier, or defense normally made by an attacking army. In our case, the attacking army is Satan the hacker and his demonic hierarchy as mentioned in Ephesians 6. Their job is to cause our spiritual hedge to be broken causing a breach in our lives, we read this in the book of Proverbs about how contaminated words cause a breach in our spirit.

> *"A wholesome tongue is a tree of life: But perverseness therein is a breach in the spirit."*

> **—Proverbs 15:4 KJV**

Perverse corrupt words overwhelm, depress, and crush our spirit, but a soothing tongue is gentle; it can soothe, build up, and encourage. It's important to speak kind words to heal and help the crushed spirit. In Isaiah 58, as God speaks about the type of fast he desires, he ensures that if we fast according to his word, we can be restorers of the breach. We can help restore every breach to heal the wounded soul.

Like the debugging process that's done in software development, our soul has to go through deliverance to clean the bugs (*demons*) that inhabited us, and a lot of times, they've come in via contaminated words. If debugging isn't done, it prevents the correct operation of computer programs, software, or systems. So likewise, when unclean spirits intrude into our souls, it can prevent us from operating as God intended.

Like a potter, God formed and molded man's body, which He made

> *"And the LORD God formed man of the dust of the ground and breathed into his nostrils the breath of life, and man became a living soul."*

> **—Genesis 2:7**

Next, God breathed His breath, the breath of life, into man's nostrils. It was the breath of God that brought forth life and made Adam lively and active. God's breath of life is like the operating system of a computer. A desktop computer with no operating system is inoperable. The breath of life made man a living soul. It is the human consciousness, mind, will, and desires. Mankind became an individual, complete in body and spirit. The "Ruach of God" is the Hebrew word for spirit, breath, or wind. When God breathed His Ruach into Adam, He breathed His will and purpose within him. His operating system caused Adam to become a living being; Adam was no longer just a form of clay.

Like the process of software development, God created man and woman and breathed His breath of life into them as His perfect creation. No debugging was necessary; God's words and purpose were within Adam & Eve. His purpose and intent for His creation were perfectly defined until the hacker, Satan corrupted their source code. He spoke the words to Eve, asking her "If God commanded them not to eat from the tree." These words implanted doubt which led to rebellion in Eve. She was under the serpent's influencing power which caused her to influence her husband. Adam should have obeyed the words of God, but he listened to the woman's voice which caused them to take on opposite roles.

As a result, the roles of Adam & Eve were reversed. In this role reversal, Adam obeyed the voice of Eve, and she became dominant; this was not the original plan of God. When something is reversed, it begins to go in the opposite direction. In this case, Adam & Eve became contrary to their creator.

Something contrary is opposite in nature, direction, or meaning. Satan was contrary and sowed discord which caused him to be removed from God's celestial network. Delayed obedience and disobedience are some signs of being contrary. After receiving clear directions in the garden, to be "fruitful, multiply, and fill the earth," Adam & Eve disobeyed God. Instead, they gave their dominion of the earth to Satan. Adam & Eve went in the opposite direction, causing them to become non-productive devices. Non-productivity means someone or something is not producing the thing they are meant to be producing. Loss of identity is what causes non-productivity in our lives.

CHAPTER 4

DISJOINTED (*IDENTITY*)

> *"So God created man in his own image, in the image of God created he him; male and female created he them. And God blessed them, and God said unto them, Be fruitful, and multiply, and replenish the earth, and subdue it: and have dominion over the fish of the sea, and over the fowl of the air, and over every living thing that moveth upon the earth."*
>
> **—Genesis 1:27–28**

God created us in His image, so we should find our identity in Him. When God created males and females, His blessing was upon them. In this proper order is how fruitfulness & multiplication comes. A Godly identity is founded and rooted in Christ Jesus. When our identity is lost, we look for it in external things. Seeking an identity on earth is like vapor. External things: relationships, careers, reputation, looks, etc., will never satisfy or define our true being because these things are superficial. It is rooted and founded upon the earth and only subject to Satan's terrestrial kingdom. As we read the New

Testament, we find out that our true identity is hidden *"In Christ."*

When we are born again, we receive a new nature and identity in Christ. We begin to understand all things will work together for our good because we are called according to his purpose (*Rom 8:28*). In Jesus, we have redemption through his blood and the forgiveness of sins (*Eph 1:17*). In Christ, our old nature is being crucified, delivering us from the power of sin. Most importantly, we are:

- A chosen people.
- A royal priesthood.
- A holy nation.
- God's special possession, He called us out of darkness into His wonderful light.

God wants us to know who we are in Christ Jesus; therefore, we will become productive and produce good works.

> *"For we are His workmanship [His own masterwork, a work of art], created in Christ Jesus [reborn from above—spiritually transformed, renewed, ready to be used] for good works, which God prepared [for us] beforehand [taking paths which He set], so that we would walk in them [living the good life which He prearranged and made ready for us]."*
>
> **—Ephesians 2:10 AMP**

Corrupt identity (Non-Productivity Hack)

"For I know the plans and thoughts that I have for you,'
says the Lord, 'plans for peace and well-being and not for
disaster, to give you a future and a hope."

—Jeremiah 29:11 AMP

Disjointed Defined: To disturb the cohesion or organization of something or anything lacking a coherent sequence or connection.

Synonyms: Unconnected, disconnected, disunited, fragmented, disorganized, disordered, incoherent, wandering, and confused.

As mentioned in chapter one, a disjointed device is a device where the primary naming service does not match its computer member domain name. As God's offspring, we are part of His family as His children. To walk in our Godly identity, we must be born again with the correct source code written over our lives. When we aren't born again, we become incoherent, searching for our identity that confuses our minds—having a loss of identity and not understanding God's plans, causes us to walk in paths He has not pre-arranged for us. When we are disjointed, our peace becomes corrupt.

God knows His plans for us, plans of good and not evil. The hacker gives identity through false words. His words breed confusion, and we know and understand that God is not the author of confusion, as stated in 1 Corinthians 14:33; *"For God is not the author of confusion, but of peace, as in all churches of the saints."*

In the Bible, confusion is a mixture of several things promiscuously, bringing disorder and irregularity. Confusion is also a blending or confounding that brings an indistinct combination instead of distinctiveness or insight. Finally, confusion brings shame and degradation, causing feelings of guilt and embarrassment. Homosexuality, lesbianism, and feelings of inadequacy come from confusion. These are some of the lies Satan has sown into the hearts of mankind to corrupt their minds.

Gender identity confusion is prevalent in our society. There is a lot of confusion centered around the proper definition of a male and female in our society today. Although God has properly defined what and who we are as males and females, our present culture has strayed far from God's original design, causing identity and gender confusion. As a result, the original command to be fruitful, multiply and replenish the earth has not been obeyed, causing God's creation to become non-productive.

Everything created by God can reproduce: plants, trees, animals, etc. A male is a gender that produces seeds with which a female may be fertilized or inseminated to produce offspring. These roles are the same with humans and in the animal kingdom. Males carry the seed, and females have the egg. This is how God created us from the beginning of time. Anything outside this natural order does not come from God but from the hacker Satan. Two of the same kind cannot reproduce; naturally, this is outside of God's order. Males cannot become females nor vice versa. Anytime, this identity is skewed; it is bred from the confusion that is not of God.

Masked Identity

> *"For nothing is hidden, except to be revealed; nor has anything been kept secret, but that it would come to light [that is, things are hidden only temporarily until the appropriate time comes for them to be known]."*
>
> **—Mark 4:22 AMP**

Masking is a process by which a person changes or "masks" their natural personality to conform to social pressures, abuse, or harassment. Masking can be strongly influenced by environmental factors such as authoritative parents, rejection, and emotional, physical, or sexual abuse. An individual may not even know they are masking because it is a behavior that can take many forms.

Jesus came to earth as manifested light, and there is no darkness in Him. Anything hidden or concealed blocks access which stops deliverance from being administered in the individual's life. When someone is masking their personality, they are operating in falsehood. When we are disjointed, we begin to lose our identity, and we are being led by the spirit of this world, we believe the lies of the hacker. Remember, Satan is a deceiver so he can only give us a false identity. Receiving our identity from the world instead of God causes us to become confused like the Devil.

He became a perversion when he disjoined God's network, like the confused identities many people have in the world today. As a result, we begin to walk down the road of reprobation, leading to moral, physical, and sexual perversion. The shame and guilt from our sin can cause us to mask our identity and live in a fake reality. Living in a simulated reality is like living in a matrix; the Devil's matrix is a world filled with lies, deception, and illusions.

Instead of facing the truth, we begin to settle for a lie. This is like a spiritual placebo that always leads to a spirit of fantasy. A spirit of fantasy causes us to be unhappy with the truth. It drives our minds to escape to the realm of fantasy and make-believe. Spiritually escaping to this place, we begin to find pleasure in what makes us feel good, whether romance novels, soap operas, pornography, sports, video games, food, shopping, sexual sin, or religious fantasy. We begin to find comfort in the Devil's matrix to escape the truth that causes us to hide from God.

We always opt for entertainment when we live a fantasy life in the devil terrestrial kingdom/matrix. Focusing on reality brings depression & heaviness because a fantasy-stricken mind has a distorted view of reality with a life fabricated by Satan.

Normalcy is boring when we have a fantasy mind; normal life is a life operating in what God has called/created us to be. When a mind is rooted in fantasies, it's easy for the demon of memory recall to cause us to always think about happier times. For example, a wife who finds her husband boring will begin to think about happier times with an ex-lover or vice versa; this causes the inability to separate lies from the truth.

A masked identity is false; it causes lying, fabrication, deception, and deceitfulness when we operate in falsehood. In addition, if rejection, trauma, abuse, and abandonment happen in our lives, it causes individuals to construct a spiritual wall of protection around their hearts which is a defense mechanism.

Defense mechanisms happen when we ignore reality and again settle for fantasy. The truth may hurt, and we put up a wall of protection to shield ourselves from any further hurt or abuse. Our hearts have a "***Do not enter***" sign, blocking anyone from ministering to our soul. In *Proverbs 18:14,* we read about a wounded spirit, and the question is asked, "Who can bear it?"

Wounded spirits are at the core of our rejection; when we have a wounded spirit, we may have a sorrowful heart that has been broken, damaged, or stricken at some point in our lives. That particular wound or heart issue causes us to deny all access to our soul.

Satan and his demons have access to our souls through these open wounds reinforcing the lies we have believed about ourselves or others; these are spiritual strongholds. A wounded, rejected person will make vows in their mind that **no one will ever have access to hurt them again**. Rejection isn't what destroys us; it's our negative reaction to rejection that does.

The incorrect inward response to rejection is a passive response to the hurts of rejection in our lives; we tend to live behind walls and masks, hiding from others and ourselves; honestly, we don't know ourselves. Since we don't know how to "be ourselves," we're always trying to be what others want us to be. Jesus was despised and rejected, so He understands how it feels to experience rejection. He died for our sins, shortcomings, rejection, etc. Like the image of the PC that has access denied, it needs the administrator to log in and access the PC. Jesus Christ is the administrator of our soul. If we tear down our walls and give him access, He can make us whole. Jesus stands at the door of our hearts and knocks; He's still speaking His words for us to allow access. If we let Him in, we will experience perfect communion with Jesus.

> *"Behold, I stand at the door, and knock: if any man hear my voice, and open the door, I will come in to him, and will sup with him, and he with me."*
>
> **—Revelation 3:20 KJV**

Tampered Devices

> *"For You formed my innermost parts; You knit me [together] in my mother's womb. I will give thanks and praise to You, for I am fearfully and wonderfully made; Wonderful are Your works, And my soul knows it very well. My frame was not hidden from You, When I was being formed in secret, And intricately and skillfully formed [as if embroidered with many colors] in the depths of the earth. Your eyes have seen my unformed substance; And in Your book were all written The days that were appointed for me, When as yet there was not one of them [even taking shape]."*
>
> **—Psalms 139:13–16 AMP**

Data Tampering: Tampering is one of the biggest security threats web applications face. Tampering means changing or deleting a resource without authorization. A web application is an application that is accessed through a web browser over the internet. Data tampering in web applications means a way in which a hacker or a malicious user gets into a website and changes, deletes, or accesses unauthorized files. A hacker or malicious user can also tamper indirectly by using a script exploit that the hacker would get the script to execute by masking it as user input from a page or as a web link.

Due to the disobedience in the garden, our purpose was perverted. God tells us in *(Psalm 51:5)* that we are born into sin and shaped into iniquity. As a result of our corrupt identities, many people have been tampered with by Satan. We now understand he made unauthorized alterations to our source code (genetic makeup) through his words. Due to these tamperings, we currently experience the following.

- Tampered Identity
- Tampered Destinies
- Tampered Gifts & Talents
- Tampered DNA

Tampered Identity: Satan attacks our identity because we're created in God's image, form, and likeness; he works to distort our view of who we are and how we see God. He plants seeds (contaminations) of doubt, blinding our minds from understanding who we are in Christ. If we aren't careful, we can easily fall into this trap by believing the devil's lies. Satan tried the same tactic with Jesus in the wilderness; he tried to sow seeds of doubt. When he attempted to cause doubt about being the son of God, Jesus overcame his lies with the word of God. (*Luke 4:1–3*)

Tampered Destiny: God has a treasure in our earthen vessel (*2nd Corinthians 4:7*). One of the main weapons Satan uses against us is distractions. Weapons of distraction are the cares of the world, worldly pleasures, and passionate desires for other things—anything designed to cause us to remain focused on temporal affairs can be a distraction. Distractions cause the word of God to become choked out of our lives, which in return will cause unfruitfulness. If we are unfruitful, we are not walking in the ways of God; this tampers our destiny.

Tampered gifts & talents: The devil likes to defile God's gifts that He has placed within us. God gave us special skills, talents, and abilities to use for the edifying of the body of Christ. As a child of God (progeny), we can become a prodigy when connected to our Progenitor (God the Father). A prodigy is a person endowed with exceptional qualities or abilities designed for us by our creator. Again, Satan plans to cause us to pervert the gift of God and use it for his kingdom, further alienating us from God, and making us prodigal sons. Jesus was well versed in the scriptures at an early age, and when He started His ministry, He showed forth distinctive signs and wonders (healing, deliverance, etc.). He was a prodigy. We can be a prodigy as well, but first, we must reconnect to our creator to allow him to perfect the gift He's given us.

"Now there are diversities of gifts, but the same spirit. And there are differences of administrations, but the same Lord. And there are diversities of operations, but it is the same God which worketh all in all."

—1 Corinthians 12:4—6

Tampered DNA: "The fall of man was genetic. Our fall impacted the gene pool, DNA, and chromosomes. Sin wasn't just what Adam and Eve did in the Garden of Eden; it is what they became."— (The Organic Gospel).

Satan tampered with our DNA to corrupt God's creation before the flood in Noah's day. We read in Genesis 6 that fallen angels slept with human women to defile their bloodline. As a result, there were giants (Nephilim) on the earth in those days. Fallen angels sleeping with human women were the first satanic attack on our DNA; this was the cause of the great flood. Jesus warns us in the last days before his second coming; that the earth will become so corrupt that it will be like the days of Noah.

Since we are entering into the times of Noah, we notice Satan is continually working to corrupt our DNA. As he works to pollute our gene pool, instead of being made in God's image, we would be in his image. His main attack is against our blood, and if he can defile or corrupt our blood, this gives him complete access to our bloodline.

Satan is not a creator; he can only alter (pervert) what God has created. Since he has perverted God's creation, we now have a society of confusion. Women identify as men, men identify as women, and homes in a perverted order, which was not the design of God but the design of the hacker Satan.

> *"And it came to pass when men began to multiply on the face of the earth, and daughters were born unto them, that the sons of God saw the daughters of men that they were fair; and they took them wives of all which they chose. There were giants in the earth in those days; and also after that, when the sons of God came in unto the daughters of men, and they bare children to them, the same became mighty men which were of old, men of renown. And the LORD said, My Spirit shall not always strive with man, for that he also is flesh: yet his days shall be an hundred and twenty years."*
>
> **—Genesis 6:1—4**

The ultimate job of Satan is to cause us to believe his lies, which creates a false identity and causes us to go off course down an unrighteous path. His desire is for us to use all of our gifts, talents, and resources for his kingdom as we take on his perverted nature. If we continue down this road, we will be given over to a reprobate (depraved) mind, receiving the wages for our sin: DEATH! His hack of tampered identities is designed to kill us while stealing from us and destroying us. In addition, he has worked diligently to alienate our minds from God, causing our minds to remain earthly.

CHAPTER 5

TERRESTRIAL MIND VS. CELESTIAL MIND

> *"For to be carnally minded is death; but to be spiritually minded is life and peace. Because the carnal mind is enmity against God: for it is not subject to the law of God, neither indeed can be. So then they that are in the flesh cannot please God."*
>
> **—Romans 8:6—8 KJV**

As mentioned at the beginning of the book, our goal is to target your mind, your body's software. Satan targets our minds by giving us vain thoughts and imaginations; these are the viruses that have corrupted our thinking; these are the imaginations mentioned in 2nd Corinthians 10; it is designed to exalt above the knowledge of God.

What is the mind, and how can one define it? First, we must understand that the mind is spiritual, which means it's appended to our spirit. However, the brain is physical, which means it's appended to our physical body; they are two different things.

The mind is the element or complex of an individual that feels, perceives, thinks, wills, and especially reasons—***Merriam Webster.***

Our mind is the intellectual or rational faculty in man; the understanding; the intellect; the power that conceives, judges, or reasons; the entire spiritual nature; the soul—often in distinction from the body—***Bible Hub Mind.***

Synonyms for mind include intellect, intelligence, intellectual capabilities, mental capacity, brains, brainpower, wits, and power of reasoning, understanding, reasoning, judgment, sense, mentality, perception, and imagination.

Battlefield of the Mind

Our mind is the battlefield where Satan works subtly, embedding his thoughts and suggestions to cause humans to do his will. A terrestrial mind is a carnal mind. We understand that remaining carnal-minded will bring forth death. Carnality is considered the flesh as opposed to the soul or spirit. When a mind is carnal, it focuses on the external or perceived by the five carnal senses. Our mind can meditate on things above, or it can remain earthly.

Those who are carnal-minded only entertain the things of the flesh. Their meditations, thoughts, and sentiments are focused on the flesh and enamored with the world. Worldly affairs, news, the lust of the eyes, the lust of the flesh, and the pride of life are important to the carnal mind. Because of these things, the carnal mind is hostile toward God with no ability nor desire to obey the word of GOD. As a result, when our mind is carnal, it is automatically the enemy of God. Living in the flesh caters to sinful appetites and impulses which cannot please God.

> *"And I, brethren, could not speak unto you as unto spiritual, but as unto carnal, even as unto babes in Christ. I have fed you with milk, and not with meat: for hitherto ye were not able to bear it, neither yet now are ye able. For ye are yet carnal: for whereas there is among you envying, and strife, and divisions, are ye not carnal, and walk as men?"*
>
> **—1 Corinthians 3:1—3 KJV**

Arrested Software (Mind)

Further examining the terrestrial mind in the scripture above, Apostle Paul wanted to speak to the believers about spiritual things. But instead, he had to talk to them as fleshly, worldly people dominated by their human nature.

Paul called them infants in Christ. As he desired to feed them with the meat of the word of God, he had to give them milk; this church was still worldly, controlled by their impulses and sinful capacity. When something's arrested, it means it has been detained, with progression and process brought to a standstill. An arrested mind stops the individual from developing or growing into full maturity.

"Concerning this we have much to say, and it is hard to explain since you have become dull and sluggish in [your spiritual] hearing and disinclined to listen. For though by this time you ought to be teachers [because of the time you have had to learn these truths], you actually need someone to teach you again the elementary principles of God's word [from the beginning], and you have come to be continually in need of milk, not solid food. For everyone who lives on milk is [doctrinally inexperienced and] unskilled in the word of righteousness, since he is a spiritual infant. But solid food is for the [spiritually] mature, whose senses are trained by practice to distinguish between what is morally good and what is evil."

—Hebrews 5:11—14 AMP

People with arrested minds can't hear, and they are unwilling to listen, making them unteachable; they are ever learning, but they can never come to the ***recognition*** of Jesus. Recognition is the ability to retain knowledge/understanding of something or someone you've encountered. The five carnal senses make the arrested mind concrete, meaning it cannot see beyond the natural; this keeps it frozen.

An arrested mind is like a device with an old software version; without the latest updates, some features are inoperative. As such, if we aren't receiving continual updates from the mind of

Christ, we will remain arrested as well. God desires our minds to be stable and continually set on heavenly things.

> *"Set your mind and keep focused habitually on the things above [the heavenly things], not on things that are on the earth [which have only temporal value]. For you died [to this world], and your [new, real] life is hidden with Christ in God. When Christ, who is our life, appears, then you also will appear with Him in glory. So put to death and deprive of power the evil longings of your earthly body [with its sensual, self-centered instincts] immorality, impurity, sinful passion, evil desire, and greed, which is [a kind of] idolatry [because it replaces your devotion to God]."*
>
> **—Colossians 3:2—5 AMP**

An unstable mind

If our minds are not settled or fixed on the things above, they will begin to wander and float; this happens because the mind is spiritual; just like any spirit, it's unseen but moves like the wind. We cannot see the wind, but we know it can blow in different directions; our minds can become the same way. So a floating mind becomes unfocused, causing it to drift from a settled state.

When our minds drift, they can become swayed by every wind of distraction. Distraction means to pull at things in two different ways or to pull asunder. When the mind is distracted, it becomes divided within its thoughts, and this is problematic because our minds shouldn't think of two things at once. *Matthew 6:34* warns us to take no thought for tomorrow, meaning we are not to take our attention from today's work to become anxious about tomorrow; sufficient for today is the evil we face.

God commands us not to be double-minded, which causes us to be blown in every direction helplessly. Instead, we have to keep our minds firm and focused on the daily affairs God has given us. Hence why Jesus Christ gives us daily bread; He wants us to live our lives daily with our minds set on Him without wavering or wondering. But unfortunately, Satan uses the weapon of distraction to divide our minds, causing us to focus on those around us and what we see instead of the demonic forces in the unseen realm. When distracted, our focus is taken off God and placed on our circumstances. As a result, we begin to doubt and worry.

We also read about this when Peter and the disciples were in the boat; he was brave enough to step out. His eyes fixed on Jesus when the command came to "*Come*" he was walking in faith toward Jesus; however when Peter saw the storm's effects, he became frightened and doubtful. Jesus asked him, "O you of little faith, why did you doubt?" Meaning he allowed himself to be drawn in two directions. (*Matthew 14:27—31*)

Divided thoughts cause our minds to become scattered, distracted, and burdened by the affairs of this world. When we have hope in this world, it will always lead to misery. A scattered mind is the same as the double mind mentioned in scripture.

When our minds are scattered and divided, this is an example of a schizophrenic mind.

> *"[For being as he is]* **a man of two minds** *(hesitating, dubious, irresolute), [he is] unstable and unreliable and uncertain about everything [he thinks, feels, decides]."*
>
> **—James 1:8 AMPC**

Schizophrenia is defined as "a long-term mental disorder involving a breakdown between thought, emotion, and behavior, leading to faulty perception, inappropriate actions and feelings, withdrawal from reality and personal relationships into fantasy and delusion, and a sense of mental fragmentation."

A schizophrenic mind is a fragmented mind that causes disturbances in the thought processes. As a result, the mind becomes impaired, making it hard to assemble data into logical, coherent ideas. Schizophrenia is another term for double-mindedness; translated means "**two minds.**"

A double-minded person is unstable and unreliable which makes them uncertain about everything. When our mind is fragmented, it has been disjointed from God's network. Having no identity, we begin to take on the world's identity. When we access the devil's network, part of our mind can become subject to the domain it identifies with; this explains the process of fragmentation, which means our mind can break into small separate parts.

> *"Do you not know that if you continually surrender yourselves to anyone to do his will, you are the slaves of him whom you obey, whether that be to sin, which leads to death, or to obedience which leads to righteousness (right doing and right standing with God)."*
>
> **—Romans 6:16**

In Romans, we learn that if we continually surrender or yield ourselves to anyone to do its will, we become slaves of the spirit we obey. We can either yield the members of our body to sin, which leads to death, or to obedience, which leads to righteousness with God. Our minds plugged into the devil's matrix made us obedient enslaved people to sin and iniquity. We are now called to be slaves to obedience, leading to righteousness and being in right standing with God.

When we yield our minds to sin, they become scattered across different domains in the terrestrial kingdom; what we meditate on is what we become. Remember, what the mouth is to our physical body, your mind is to the spiritual body. You are what you eat!

If we continue to yield our members to these powers, it will lead to death. In short, the terrestrial mind is a carnal mind that leads to death, first spiritually and ultimately physically. The goal of the carnal mind is to keep you and I focused on the affairs of this world, never meditating on things above. Therefore, it's time to crucify the carnal mind! So, saints, we must update the operating system in our minds. God desires us to come up higher and plug into His network, no longer arrested by the appetites of this world nor wandering in the devil's kingdom. It's time to think heavenly thoughts.

Celestial (Heavenly) mind

"Therefore, if you have been raised with Christ [to a new life, sharing in His resurrection from the dead], keep seeking the things that are above, where Christ is, seated at the right hand of God. Set your mind and keep focused habitually on the things above [the heavenly things], not on things that are on the earth [which have only temporal value]. For you died [to this world], and your [new, real] life is hidden with Christ in God. When Christ, who is our life, appears, then you also will appear with Him in glory."

—Colossians 3:1–4 AMP

A celestial mind is constantly seeking after things above. The things which are above are what is upward, above the brim, and high up. Jesus Christ and God our Father are above; therefore, the heavenly mind exercises sentiments for only Godly affairs. Exercising our mind to only meditate on celestial matters means our mind is dead to the affairs of this world and hidden with Christ in God.

Setting our minds on things above is the same as setting our hearts on heavenly things. It is all about God's will being done on earth, as it is in Heaven. When our minds meditate on the things above, they will be kept peaceful. So we read in Isaiah that God keeps us in perfect peace when our minds stay on him.

> *"You will keep in perfect and constant peace the one whose mind is steadfast [that is, committed and focused on You—in both inclination and character] Because he trusts and takes refuge in You [with hope and confident expectation]."*

—Isaiah 26:3

The Crucified Mind

A steadfast mind is loyal, faithful, committed, and devoted to God. When our minds are heavenly, they will have refuge in God as our hiding place. As a result, there is no fear, anxiety, doubts, or worrying because our hope and confident expectation are in God instead of this world. When we begin to worry or become anxious, we can assure ourselves that we have disconnected from God's divine network.

However, we will have a settled, made-up mind when we crucify our minds. Jesus had a settled mind after His battle in the garden of Gethsemane. As He continually prayed in the garden, He was in agony. Finally, knowing that He was facing His death, He told the Father, "Not my will, but Your Will be done;" Jesus' mind was resolute about doing the Father's will. We must be adamant in our mind about obeying the Father as well.

> *"So they took Jesus, and He went out, bearing His own cross, to the place called the Place of the Skull, which is called in Hebrew, Golgotha. There they crucified Him*

> *and with Him two others, one on either side and Jesus between them. Pilate also wrote an inscription [on a placard] and put it on the cross. And it was written: 'JESUS THE NAZARENE, THE KING OF THE JEWS.'"*
>
> **—John 19:17–19 AMP**

Jesus bearing His cross went to the place of the skull, which is called Golgotha. His crucifixion at Golgotha is important because it shows how we must crucify our fleshly/carnal minds—killing the old man with all of his lusts and passions. If we desire a settled mind, we must first crucify the old man (mind). Crucifixion means to be nailed to a cross or executed. Jesus understood this importance which is why he went to Calvary, the place of the skull. In the natural body, the skull is the part that encloses the brain. So, if we desire to live a resurrected life focused on heavenly things, we must begin crucifying our fleshly minds and all the carnal inputs that enclose them; this means we are no longer alive to sin, but now we are alive to God.

> *"Knowing this, that our old man is crucified with him that the body of sin might be destroyed, that henceforth we should not serve sin."*
>
> **—Romans 6:6**

Purity of mind

> *"Finally, believers, whatever is true, whatever is honorable and worthy of respect, whatever is right and confirmed by God's word, whatever is pure and wholesome, whatever is lovely and brings peace, whatever is admirable and of good repute; if there is any excellence, if there is anything worthy of praise, think continually on these things [center your mind on them, and implant them in your heart]. The things which you have learned and received and heard and seen in me, practice these things [in daily life], and the God [who is the source] of peace and well-being will be with you."*
>
> **—Philippians 4:8–9 AMP**

When we are alive to God, we can meditate on what's pure. The spirit of our mind must have the correct operating system. If we are not meditating on the things of God, our minds will be plugged into the devil's network, bound by the perversion and filth of the world. In scripture, we're admonished to meditate on honorable things; that is anything confirmed by the word of God. Again, we have to exercise the mind to think and meditate on the right things and put them into practice. In Hebrews 5:14, we read that solid food (the pure word of God) brings us to spiritual maturity. When we meditate on pure words, we will begin to exercise our senses to discern between good and evil. Meditating on God's word helps us understand the hacker's evil works and see them more clearly. Our mind will eat anything we feed it; as such, we have to provide it with pure thoughts and pure words, not allowing ungodly thinking that can lead to sin. When we are drawn away by our temptation, James warns us that it is not of God but of the devil. The process of temptation starts in our minds. When we meditate on the temptation, we can be drawn away by lust, and when this lust is conceived, it brings forth sin, and sin when finished, brings forth death. (James 1:15) because of this, we need to reload the operating system of our minds. We need a fresh install.

CHAPTER 6

RELOADING THE NETWORK

> *"if so be that ye have heard him, and have been taught by him, as the truth is in Jesus: that ye put off concerning the former conversation the old man, which is corrupt according to the deceitful lusts; and be renewed in the spirit of your mind..."*
>
> **—Ephesians 4:21–23 KJV**

It's time to reload the software of our minds. Whenever an operating system is reloaded, it could be due to a hard drive crash, malware, or any corruption or failure experienced. We understand that our old man (nature) was corrupt with his deceitful lusts and desires; as a result, we must undergo a reload/renewal of the mind to remove the old corrupt nature. Our characteristics of the old nature show that we were corrupt in our ways with a delusional mind.

All of our belief systems, strongholds, and perceptions must be washed away by the word of God. This process is a constant renewal of the spirit of our minds, which allows us to have a fresh mental and spiritual attitude. As we continue renewing our minds after being born again, reading the Bible daily, and exercising our senses to discern between what is good and evil, we will begin to walk in our new nature organically. Our new nature is the regenerated nature created in God's image, which makes us Godlike in true righteousness and holiness. As we are made more into God's image, we begin to reject all falsity and delusions and live in the truth.

We are not to be conformed to the pattern of this world (Rom 12:2), nor fashion ourselves after the worldly systems with their superficial customs. Instead, we must be transformed (changed) by the renewal of our minds. When we have a renewed mind, we can prove and understand God's good, acceptable, and perfect will, even understanding what is good, acceptable, and perfect in His sight. But, first, we must present our bodies to our Creator; this process is the same for any device that has experienced corruption.

Like giving our computer or smartphone to the technician to receive repairs, we as born-again believers must submit our bodies (devices) to God as a living sacrifice. God wants us to present all of ourselves, set apart, and be dedicated to Him; this is holy and well-pleasing to God and our reasonable service and act of worship. God wants all of us as a complete sacrifice; this will allow Him to repair and recreate us into the image of His Son, Jesus Christ. Therefore, we must yield to the process of transformation.

As we continue in God's presence, the viruses that the devil has implanted will be removed. We have the blood of Jesus that will cleanse us and make us pure. God restores our soul (mind). The key to restoration is accessing God's network by staying in His presence. God's mind is orderly, logical, and on time. He expects His offspring to function similarly, having our minds renewed to function in this orderly way. We must first plug into the power of God's network.

CHAPTER 7

POWER OF THE CELESTIAL NETWORK

> *"But ye shall receive power, after that the Holy Ghost is come upon you: and ye shall be witnesses unto me both in Jerusalem, and in all Judæa, and in Samaria, and unto the uttermost part of the earth."*
>
> **—Acts 1:8 KJV**

In God's celestial network, the Holy Ghost is the power supply. A power supply is an essential component for a computer; without a power supply, the computer is only a box of hardware. It has great potential but without a power source, the potential cannot be accessed. It is the power supply that converts alternating current (AC) to direct current (DC) that is needed by the personal computer. As such, we need to plug into God's network through which the Holy Ghost will bring forth the conversion we need to operate in God's kingdom.

The book of Acts shows the acts of the Holy Ghost. In the scripture above, Jesus, speaking to the disciples, promised them that they will receive power and ability when the Holy Spirit comes upon them. When we receive the Baptism of the Holy Ghost, we will become witnesses to tell others about Jesus. The power mentioned in this scripture is "Dunamis," a Greek word that means "force." *Romans 1:16* shows that the Gospel of Jesus Christ is the dunamis of God to salvation for everyone who believes. The dunamis is also the miraculous power of God which gives us the ability and might to do the will of God allowing us to become effective witnesses (martyrs) for Jesus Christ.

When you become a witness for Jesus, this means when the Holy Spirit comes upon us we die, completely to our old ways. Any of our selfish motives, indulgences, or inadequacies is dead, and our life as a witness is lived out to manifest the glory of God even unto death. Stephen is an example of an effective witness, he was completely transformed and spoke the truth of the gospel which caused him to become a martyr. Jesus Christ was well pleased with Stephen, He stands at the right hand of the Father to welcome His faithful witness. He was a good and faithful servant (*Acts 7–8*).

The Ministry of the Spirit

The Holy Spirit is a real person; He is the Spirit of God. The Holy Ghost has been given to us as our comforter, advocate, intercessor, counselor, strengthener, and standby. He teaches us all things and also brings to mind and remembrance the word of God. As children of God, our body is a temple of the Holy Spirit, which means we are not our own property. The Holy Spirit is within us as a gift from God; however, He is only given to those who obey. He is the Spirit of Truth, which means when we are connected to God's network and filled with the Holy Spirit, we will begin to put aside all delusions and walk in the truth. The world cannot receive the Holy Spirit because the world doesn't see Him or know Him. Remember, the terrestrial kingdom is built upon lies and delusion, which is why those led by the spirit of the world cannot receive the Spirit of Truth because they walk in error.

The Holy Spirit guides us into the complete truth. He doesn't speak on His own initiative, He speaks what He hears from God the Father regarding Jesus Christ. The Holy Ghost magnifies Jesus. When we are filled with the Holy Ghost, we experience true freedom from bondage. As we continue walking with Jesus Christ, we will begin to grow the fruit of the Spirit in our lives, which comes from our connection with the Holy Spirit. God's life flows through our fellowship with the Holy Spirit. Walking in communion with the Holy Spirit is like being a battery or a capacitor charged with electrical current.

We can get so full of God's power that when we speak or act, there's a spark *Mark 16:15–20* gives a great example of this. When we are led and full of the Holy Spirit, we will have the ability to preach the gospel, and when we believe, some signs will follow us.

"And these signs shall follow them that believe; In my name shall they cast out devils; they shall speak with new tongues; they shall take up serpents; and if they

drink any deadly thing, it shall not hurt them; they shall lay hands on the sick, and they shall recover."

—Mark 16:17–18 KJV

Prayer is how we communicate with the Holy Spirit. In God's celestial network, it's through prayers that we keep being in constant communication with our Father. God hears our prayers, and His ears are attentive to our prayers. When we pray, we can pray for others, ourselves, and whoever the Lord places upon our hearts. Jesus is our example of an intercessor, He spent His time in prayer when He was here on earth, and He is still interceding on our behalf.

Prayer, the Catalyst

"Confess your faults one to another and pray one for another, that ye may be healed. The effectual fervent prayer of a righteous man availeth much."

—James 5:16

Prayer is the catalyst for our breakthroughs. In the book of Acts, the visions, miracles, healings, and deliverance were put into action by prayer and worship. Prayer is the offering of our desires to God through the name of Jesus Christ; it is also the communion of the heart as guided by the Holy Spirit. When we pray, we offer petitions, requests, and supplications. Building a steady communication with God in prayer, we begin to seek, ask, and entreat God on behalf of our affairs while here on earth. In the book of James, we are advised to pray for one another. This is an act of intercession, which is intervening on behalf of another. Effectual prayer is effective, successful, and powerful. It is productive and brings forth fruit. These are the fruitful prayers the church was offering on behalf of Peter when he was in prison.

> *"So Peter was kept in prison, but fervent and persistent prayer for him was being made to God by the church. When he had seized Peter, he put him in prison, turning him over to four squads of soldiers of four each to guard him [in rotation throughout the night], planning after the Passover to bring him out before the people [for execution]."*

> **—Acts 12:4–5**

The prayer the church offered to God was prayer and worship by supplication. The church offered a fervent and persistent prayer on behalf of Peter. Fervent means to be ardent, earnest, full of zeal, and hot. As a result of this type of prayer, God delivered Peter from prison. He heard the prayer of the Saints!

Power from on High

> *"And when the day of Pentecost was fully come, they were all with one accord in one place. And suddenly there came a sound from heaven as of a rushing mighty wind, and it filled all the house where they were sitting.*

> *And there appeared unto them cloven tongues like as of fire, and it sat upon each of them. And they were all filled with the Holy Ghost, and began to speak with other tongues, as the Spirit gave them utterance."*
>
> **—Acts 2:1–4**

"During Pentecost, the believers were together in one place. Suddenly, a sound came from heaven like a violent rushing wind; it filled the house where they were sitting. Tongues of **FIRE** appeared, which were distributed among the believers and rested on each of them. Just like the power supply of a machine the Holy Ghost gives us power from on high to be effective in His kingdom. Immediately after the church received the baptism of the Holy Spirit, Peter preached his first sermon, resulting in more than 3,000 souls being added to the body of believers." *Acts 2:40–41*

God's celestial network is powered by the Holy Ghost, and it contains all the provisions necessary to prosper in this life. This example is shown in the scripture above where Peter was able to convert 3,000 souls into the body of Christ. When we are connected to the network of God, we can abide in the vine. All the sap in the tree will give us the power to become fruitful in our lives.

Abiding in the Network

> *"I am the true vine, and my Father is the husbandman. Every branch in me that beareth not fruit he taketh away: and every branch that beareth fruit, he purgeth it, that it may bring forth more fruit. Now ye are clean through the word which I have spoken unto you. Abide in me, and I in you. As the branch cannot bear fruit of itself, except it abide in the vine; no more can ye, except ye abide in me. I am the vine, ye are the branches: He that abideth in me, and I in him, the same bringeth forth much fruit: for without me ye can do nothing. If a man abide not in me, he is cast forth as a branch, and is withered; and men gather them, and cast them into the fire, and they are burned. If ye abide in me, and my words abide in you, ye shall ask what ye will, and it shall be done unto you. Herein is my Father glorified, that ye bear much fruit; so shall ye be my disciples."*
>
> **—John 15:1–8 KJV**

God's celestial network is expressed in *John 15*, as Jesus speaks to the disciples about abiding in the vine. Jesus Christ is the vine, which means He is the support. We are the branches of the vine if we stay in connection with Jesus. This means we are to dwell, endure, and remain in His network so that we will bear much fruit organically, transforming into the image and likeness of Jesus Christ.

If we disconnect from God's network, we are cutting ourselves off from vital union (connection) with Jesus, and thus will not be able to accomplish anything. Prayer, Bible study, fasting, and cultivating a relationship with God keep us in vital union (connection) to His network. The device that disconnects from God's network is considered inoperative and will be thrown out like a broken-off branch. If we remain disconnected from Jesus, our support, we will wither and die. These are the devices that are continually joined to Satan's kingdom and being prepared for the fire of Judgment. God's power is not demonstrated in the lives of those that remain non-interactive with the Holy Ghost. It is imperative that we listen and obey the instructions given to us, cooperating with God's network to do His will.

We remain in Jesus through His words remaining in us. The word of God is the source code that recalibrates our minds, keeping us vitally united to our source. Since we are in vital union with Jesus, we can ask whatever we wish in accordance with the will of God, and it will be done for us. In this connection, God our Father is glorified and honored because we are bearing fruit and proving ourselves to be true disciples of Jesus Christ. Plug into God's powerful celestial network and allow the power to flow through you! As the world grows darker, the Church shines brighter. We will do miraculous exploits to show hopeless blinded people that Jesus Christ is real and desires to save them from this present evil age. Always remember, the network is the POWER!

CHAPTER 8

ASCENSION OF THE CELESTIAL NETWORK

> *"There are also celestial bodies, and bodies terrestrial: but the glory of the celestial is one, and the glory of the terrestrial is another."*
>
> **—1 Corinthians 15:40**

Transition into Resurrection

Jesus is the resurrection and the life. Something that is resurrected is raised from the dead and restored to life. Resurrection brings revival, restoration, regeneration, and rebirth. We can live the resurrected life NOW by dying to our old man and being resurrected to the newness of life in Christ Jesus because we have been quickened together with Jesus and seated in Heavenly places.

> *"Even when we were dead in sins, hath quickened us together with Christ, (by grace ye are saved;) and hath*

> *raised us up together, and made us sit together in heavenly places in Christ Jesus...*"
>
> **—Ephesians 2:5–6 AMP**

Whoever believes in, adheres to, trusts in, and relies on Jesus as Savior will live in eternity. Jesus Christ is the key to eternity, and in Him is found resurrected life.

There are celestial and terrestrial bodies. A celestial body is heavenly which means it is above the sky in the heavens while a terrestrial body remains upon the earth and is earthly. This is the same with the resurrection of the dead. Our human body can perish and is mortal, but when our human body is raised, it will become imperishable and immortal. When our bodies ascend to the heavens, we will put off all dishonor and be raised in glory.

Our natural body will be raised as a spiritual body that will be suited for heaven. As we read about Adam in the book of Genesis, Adam was the first man. He became a living soul which means he was earthly. Jesus Christ came as our Savior to save us from this world. He was our last Adam, and He became a life-giving Spirit, which means He restores the dead to life. God sent His only begotten Son Jesus Christ, as the door (*portal*) through which we must enter to be saved. When we enter through Jesus, we will have spiritual security. He is the only doorway to the realm of eternal life spent with God our Father. If we try to enter any other way, we are considered thieves and robbers. Restoration from death to life happens when we are born again, transforming to be changed from one life type to another.

Caterpillars & Butterflies: The Process of Transformation

Transformation is a metamorphosis that takes place when our minds are changed from one life type to another. A transformed mind is likened to a butterfly, as opposed to a caterpillar, which represents a terrestrial, earthly mind. A caterpillar and a butterfly have the same beginning, but only through metamorphosis can a caterpillar become a butterfly. It is the same with us. When we are born, we are all born into sin and molded into iniquity. Everyone has the potential to be a butterfly because it is already inside of us.

Caterpillars are earthbound, stuck to the ground, and unable to see up high. Those with a caterpillar mind desire to be something in the world and are willing to conform to be accepted in the terrestrial kingdom. They must go through a metamorphosis by changing life types through an organic transformation from one species to another. This is the process of being born again.

Someone with a butterfly mind is born again. They are metamorphosed from an earthbound species of a caterpillar and begin to take on the character of God with the mind of Christ. This is where the conflict comes in because we are no longer plugged into the devil's network with a carnal mind. Instead, we are now connected to God's network with the mind of Christ. To become a butterfly, we must sanctify ourselves. In this case, the cocoon is necessary to metamorphose from the life of a caterpillar to a butterfly.

The cocoon process

To become a butterfly, a caterpillar first digests itself. One day, the caterpillar stops eating, hangs upside down from a twig or leaf, and spins itself into a silky cocoon or molts into a shiny chrysalis. Within its protective casing, the caterpillar radically transforms its body, eventually emerging as a butterfly or moth. This allows the caterpillar to go through a radical transformation. Some caterpillars walk around with tiny wings inside but we will never know it by looking at them. They must enter the cocoon to metamorphose. (***Scientific American***)

This is how transformation happens as a born-again Christian, through denying ourselves of our selfish desires. Just as a caterpillar must deny itself of food, wrap itself in a cocoon, and totally shut out the world until it has been fully transformed, we must also deny ourselves through fasting, wrap ourselves tight with prayer and the word of God, and completely shut out the world until we are fully transformed. The Bible calls this process sanctification unto holiness, and it, by nature, produces in us the ascended mind of a butterfly.

The Ascended Mind

"Who may ascend onto the mountain of the Lord? And who may stand in His holy place? He who has clean hands and a pure heart, Who has not lifted up his soul to what is false, Nor has sworn [oaths] deceitfully. He shall receive a blessing from the Lord, And righteousness from the God of his salvation.

> *This is the generation (description) of those who diligently seek*
> *Him and require Him as their greatest need, Who seek Your face,*
> *even [as did] Jacob. Selah. "*
>
> **—Psalms 24:3–6**

The word "ascension" describes the act of rising through the air. Ascension is also the act of rising to an important position or a higher level like the butterfly. Mount Zion is the city of God, and there is where our minds should ascend to. When our minds are ascended to the City of God, we will begin to stand/dwell in His Holy Place. Scripture tells us that we must have clean hands and a pure heart, no longer lift our souls to lies and deceit, and no longer walk in agreement with the Hacker (Satan) who is a deceiver. Those who desire to live the ascended life will receive the blessing of eternal life from God. Now is the time, Saints. We are the generation that is called to diligently seek the Lord and require Him as our greatest need, seeking His face to understand His will and purpose for our lives. We must be rejoined back to the Father's network through His Son Jesus Christ. Our God is a God of suddenly; soon, we will all be completely changed, wondrously transformed in a moment, in the twinkling of an eye, at the sound of the last trumpet call. Will you answer the call?

> *"The earth is the LORD's, and the fulness thereof; The*
> *world, and they that dwell therein. For he hath founded*
> *it upon the seas, And established it upon the floods. Who*
> *shall ascend into the hill of the LORD? Or who shall*
> *stand in his holy place? He that hath clean hands, and a*

pure heart; Who hath not lifted up his soul unto vanity, nor sworn deceitfully. He shall receive the blessing from the LORD, And righteousness from the God of his salvation. This is the generation of them that seek him, That seek thy face, O Jacob. Selah. Lift up your heads, O ye gates; And be ye lifted up ye everlasting doors; And the King of glory shall come in. Who is this King of glory? The LORD strong and mighty, the LORD mighty in battle. Who is this King of glory? The LORD of hosts, he is the King of glory. Selah. Lift up your heads, O ye gates; even lift them up, ye everlasting doors; And the King of glory shall come in."

—Psalm 24:1–10 KJV

Friends, join us on this celestial journey as we seek to find and fulfill our destinies in God's kingdom. Jesus Christ has come to set captive souls free, liberating us from Satan's plan to damn our souls eternally to hell. The Lord has provided us with a way to escape the mental enslavement the devil used to make us non-productive, useless, hypnotized zombies, living only to do his perverse, insidious will. It's time for us to break out of his spell and move on to the higher ground. As saints of God, spread your wings and fly high like eagles to join us in God's magnificent celestial network! God bless you and keep you is our prayer.

Deliverance Prayer

Father God, we thank you for this word; we submit this time to you, Lord, and ask that you will cleanse our minds. Lord, we understand the hacking of the minds which has been happening since the fall of man. Therefore, I ask You, Father, to help me be cleansed and renewed in the spirit of my mind.

Heavenly Father, we confess and repent where we have given Satan access to our minds. I break agreement with Satan and his demonic kingdom, with every spirit of arrested development, mind control, schizophrenia, and rejection. God, I want to be renewed in the spirit of my mind; please help me transform my mind by meditating on Your word as I continually seek You. Father, help me to receive deliverance from the mind of the flesh, and please teach me how to put on the mind of Christ. I pray that You will restore my fragmented mind; wherever it has been scattered, broken, or split; Your word promises to restore my soul/mind.

Lord, as I continue to seek You, I pray that You will give me a steadfast and peaceful mind that is committed and focused on You. Show me how to apply my mind to the knowledge of GOD so that I can KNOW You more.

Finally, Father, I pray that You will help me have a made-up mind. So that I can take a definitive stand about serving You, no longer being double-minded, and allow me to be persuaded about my relationship with You.

Lord, let Your peace stand guard over my mind. I thank You, Father, for receiving and answering this prayer. I give You praise both now and forever in Jesus's name AMEN!

> *"You will keep in perfect and constant peace the one whose mind is steadfast [that is, committed and focused on You—in both inclination and character] Because he trusts and takes refuge in You [with hope and confident expectation]."*
>
> **—Isaiah 26:3 AMP**

References

"Masking (Personality)." *Wikipedia*, Wikimedia Foundation, 8 Mar. 2022, https://en.m.wikipedia.org/wiki/Masking (personality).

"What Is a Hacker?" *Study.com | Take Online Courses. Earn College Credit. Research Schools, Degrees & Careers*, https://study.com/academy/lesson/what-is-a-hacker-definition-lesson-quiz.html

"Data Tampering - Meaning, Types and Countermeasures." *MBA Knowledge Base*, 3 Sept. 2018, https://www.mbaknol.com/information-systems-management/data-tampering-meaning-types-and-countermeasures/

"What is a Computer Virus?" https://us.norton.com/internet security-malware-what-is-a-computer-virus.html

"What is Data Corruption" - https://en.wikipedia.org/wiki/Data corruption

"Black hat Hacker" https://www.kaspersky.com/resource-center/definitions/hacker-hat-types

"Schizophrenia"https://studydriver.com/schizophrenia-long-term-mental-disorder/